I Love My Pet
DOG

Aaron Carr

MEDIA ENHANCED BOOKS
AV2 BY WEIGL™
ADDED VALUE • AUDIO VISUAL

www.av2books.com

AV² provides enriched content that supplements and complements this book. Weigl's AV² books strive to create inspired learning and engage young minds in a total learning experience.

Your AV² Media Enhanced books come alive with...

Audio
Listen to sections of the book read aloud.

Key Words
Study vocabulary, and complete a matching word activity.

Go to **www.av2books.com**, and enter this book's unique code.

Video
Watch informative video clips.

Quizzes
Test your knowledge.

BOOK CODE

J738478

Embedded Weblinks
Gain additional information for research.

Slide Show
View images and captions, and prepare a presentation.

AV² by Weigl brings you media enhanced books that support active learning.

Try This!
Complete activities and hands-on experiments.

... and much, much more!

Published by AV² by Weigl
350 5th Avenue, 59th Floor New York, NY 10118
Website: www.av2books.com www.weigl.com

Library of Congress Cataloging-in-Publication Data
Carr, Aaron.
 Dog / Aaron Carr.
   p. cm. -- (I love my pet dog)
 ISBN 978-1-61690-921-5 (hardcover : alk. paper) -- ISBN 978-1-61690-567-5 (online)
 1. Dogs--Juvenile literature. I. Title.
 SF426.5.C376 2012
 636.7--dc23
                        2011024926

Printed in the United States of America in North Mankato, Minnesota
1 2 3 4 5 6 7 8 9 0 15 14 13 12 11

062011
WEP030611

Project Coordinator: Aaron Carr   Art Director: Terry Paulhus
Weigl acknowledges Getty Images, iStock, and Dreamstime as image suppliers for this title.

I Love My Pet DOG

CONTENTS

3

I love my pet dog.
I take good care of him.

5

My pet dog was a puppy.
He could not see or hear
when he was born.

My pet dog grows fast.
He will grow to full size
in one year.

The world's smallest dog
is a 4-inch tall chihuahua.

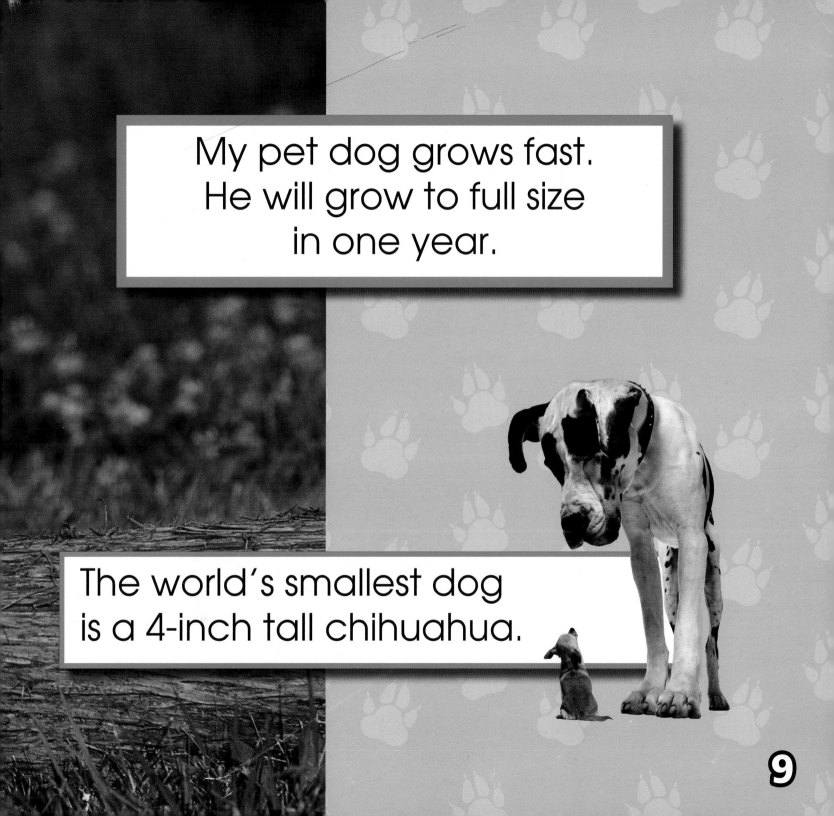

My pet dog can hear sounds
that I can not hear.
He can also turn his ears
toward a sound.

Dogs use 18 muscles
to move their ears.

My pet dog can run very fast.
He can run faster
than I can ride on my bike.

Greyhounds can run
as fast as a car.

13

14

My pet dog sleeps
up to 16 hours each day.
I try not to wake him
when he is sleeping.

My pet dog only eats
two times a day.
It is my job to give him food.

Eating chocolate
can make dogs sick.

My pet dog cleans his teeth
by chewing.
I give him bones to chew.

I help make sure
my pet dog is healthy.
I love my pet dog.

DOG FACTS

This page provides more detail about the interesting facts found in the book. Simply look for the corresponding page number to match the fact.

Pages 4–5

I love my pet dog. I take good care of him. Dogs are one of the most popular pets. About one out of every three houses in the United States has a pet dog. Dogs come in many different sizes, colors, and breeds. Keeping a pet dog is a lot of work. Dogs need regular feeding, walks, baths, and playtime.

Pages 6–7

My pet dog was a puppy. He could not see or hear when he was born. Baby dogs are called puppies. Newborn puppies need their mother to keep them safe and feed them. They cannot see, hear, or walk. Puppies also have no teeth when they are born. A puppy must be at least eight weeks old before it can go to a new home.

Pages 8–9

My pet dog grows fast. He will grow to full size in one year. Dogs mature faster than humans. A one-year-old dog is comparable to a 15-year-old person. By age 15, he is like a 76-year-old person. Dogs live 10 to 15 years. As dogs age, their needs change. A veterinarian can help make sure your dog is properly cared for in all stages of life.

Pages 10–11

My pet dog can hear sounds that I can not hear. He can also turn his ears toward a sound. Dogs can hear up to four times better than humans. Dogs can also close part of their ear to focus on a single sound. Loud noises, such as thunder or vacuum cleaners, can scare a dog and even hurt its ears.

Pages 12–13

My pet dog can run very fast. He can run faster than I can ride on my bike. Most dogs can run much faster than humans. The greyhound is the fastest dog. It can run more than 40 miles (64 kilometers) per hour. This is faster than most people can ride a bike. In general, dogs should spend 20 to 30 minutes running each day.

Pages 14–15

My pet dog sleeps up to 16 hours each day. I try not to wake him when he is sleeping. Depending on the breed, dogs can spend between 12 and 16 hours sleeping each day. Sleeping dogs should not be woken. Most dog bites occur when a sleeping dog is woken suddenly. Dogs need plenty of sleep and exercise to stay healthy.

Pages 16–17

My pet dog only eats two times a day. It is my job to give him food. Dogs should be fed at about the same time every day. They also need to drink water many times during the day. Some foods that humans eat are harmful to dogs. Foods such as chocolate, raisins, grapes, onions, and some nuts are poisonous for dogs.

Pages 18–19

My pet dog cleans his teeth by chewing. I give him bones to chew. Dogs need to chew on bones or toys to keep their teeth clean. Dogs should clean their teeth at least twice a week. It is also good for dogs to have their teeth checked by a veterinarian every year. Keeping a dog's teeth clean helps prevent many diseases.

Pages 20–21

I help make sure my pet dog is healthy. I love my pet dog. Dogs need regular checkups. Most dogs should visit a veterinarian at least once a year. Puppies should receive vaccination shots when they are about six to eight weeks old. If your dog is sick, take him to a veterinarian right away.

WORD LIST

Research has shown that as much as 65 percent of all written material published in English is made up of 300 words. These 300 words cannot be taught using pictures or learned by sounding them out. They must be recognized by sight. This book contains 55 common sight words to help young readers improve their reading fluency and comprehension. This book also teaches young readers several important content words, such as proper nouns. These words are paired with pictures to aid in learning and improve understanding.

Page	Sight Words First Appearance
5	good, him, I, my, of, take
7	a, could, he, hear, not, or, see, was, when
9	grows, in, is, one, the, to, will, world, year
11	also, can, hear, his, move, sounds, that, their, toward, turn, use
12	as, on, run, than, very
15	day, each, hours, try, up
16	eats, food, give, it, make, only, times, two
18	by
21	help

Page	Content Words First Appearance
5	dog, pet
7	puppy
9	chihuahua, size, world
11	ear, muscles, sound
12	bike, car
16	chocolate
18	bones, teeth

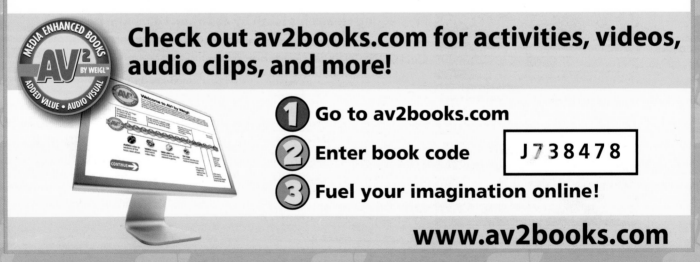